THE CALL & BURDEN OF INTERCESSORY PRAYER

Dedications

To my beloved Mother, who is making her transition to be with the Father as I write this.

Thank you Mother, for putting my feet on the path of the prophetic.

Your Son, Michael

To my dear wife, Cassandra, and my children, Michael, Angelique, Josef, Timothy and Gabriella, my grandchildren, Angela, Elijah, and Hadassah; whom allowed me to neglect them during this time.

To Truth Christian Assembly, my church family
Thank you for your persistent prayers
I Love You, Your Shepherd

To My Editor, Elder Regina Burton

Thank you for your unfailing faithfulness

THE FORWARD

The Call and the Burden of Intercessory Prayer is the outpouring of one prophet and intercessor's rallying cry for the revival and restoration of powerful prayer, especially intercessory prayer. All members of the Body of Christ are called to intercede, but there should also be a special sector in local congregations and ministries, led by the apostolic head of the local assembly, to which those specially anointed to stand in the gap for the kingdom of God, and God's saints and against the works of Satan are called. Our example for the ministry is Jesus Christ Himself, our Great High Priest. The need for the rebirth of the intercessory prayer ministry is urgent, and those now favored with the gapers anointing live in a time when the kingdom of God suffers much violence and when violent prayer warriors need to be positioned to call down the power of God. The Call and the Burden of Intercessory Prayer is a vital handbook for those desiring to understand the keys to fruitful intercessory prayer.

Bishop William H. Murphy Jr.

Table of Contents

THE INTERCESSOR QUESTION

It is clear to me that God is restoring by His Spirit the ascension gifts, better known as the five-fold ministry (Ephesians 4:11-13). With the restoration of these offices will also come the restoration of power, ability and spiritual dynamics like in the days of Elijah and Elisha. According to Joel 2:23, there is an expectation of a great outpouring of the Spirit of God – of miracles, signs and wonders in these last days. Never before has the church witnessed the calling of so many men and women to the ministry of Jesus Christ. This is also a direct sign and signal as the prophecy of Joel 2:28-32 is fulfilled – *"In the last days I will pour out My spirit on all flesh: your sons and your daughters shall prophesy..."*[1] Make no mistake that these promises of position, power, posterity and pouring out will emerge in response to intercessory prayer. Prayer must be restored. Without prayer before the throne of God, the manifestation of our greatness may be delayed. Our modern day apostles, bishops, prophets, pastors, teachers and evangelists all stand like an army ready to do battle with all the natural equipment, excellence, emotion, elegance and excitement, but without the consistent operation of intercession, they exhibit no real power - for Jesus revealed that real power comes through prayer, prayer with

---

[1] Unless otherwise noted, all Scripture quotations are from the King James Version of the Holy Bible.

fasting, prayer with earnestness, prayer with vigor and vitality, prayer that will reach heaven, prayer that will ascend up to God, causing God to respond with the fulfillment of the promise of his word, *"If My people who are called by My name will humble themselves, and pray, and seek my face, and turn from their wicked ways, then I will hear from heaven, and will forgive their sin and heal their land. Now will My eyes be open and my ears attentive to prayer made in this place"* (2 Chronicles 7:14-15).

These days, you can turn on the television and get a word for the day or a lesson for the week, and this is great – however, there are still people who, after the word is preached and the lessons are taught, are still hurting and in bondage of multi-dimensions, who are still sick and still not delivered, who need a God, a Jesus, who does more than talk. They need a Jesus who is able to *demonstrate* His presence and power. When one peruses Scripture one can easily see that God delights to display His power at the behest of an intercessor. An intercessor is one who stands in the *gap* on behalf of others. Is the church at large postured to intercede? *"So I sought for a man among them who would make a wall, and stand in the gap before me on behalf of the land, that I should not destroy it; but I found no one"* (Ezekiel 22:30).

Throughout the Bible, we find individuals who meet the biblical criteria of intercessor. In Genesis 8:20-22, Noah meets this high demand as he preserves the earth through intercessory prayer. In Genesis 18:16-33, we find righteous Abraham interceding for wicked Sodom and Gomorrah. In the book of Exodus, the prophet Moses often sought the face of God for the deliverance and salvation of his people Israel. Exodus 31:1-14 reveals his mantle as an intercessor as Moses intercedes and turns the heart of God from destroying His people for their sin.

The list continues with the likes of Daniel, Jeremiah, King David, King Solomon, the Lord's apostles and, chiefly, Christ Jesus our Lord Himself. These heralds of the faith, along with many other men and women of the Bible, prove that the work of the intercessor is always necessary. But, are intercessors *called* to this most serious work, is it the burden of the heart supernaturally imposed by the Holy Spirit, or is every believer an intercessor with various assignments and territories given to us by the Spirit of the Lord? These are important questions for the life and future state of Christendom. Do we *wait* for God to divinely *call* persons to this urgent ministry while the world continues on its collision course with mayhem and destruction? Or, rather, shall we come to recognize, as the chosen and elect people of God and servants of the Great High Priest and Intercessor, that it is our *responsibility* to take up this priestly assignment in the earth realm? If the latter is true, then woe to the pastors and ministers of every sort who pretend they are too busy for prayer and intercession by assigning this crucial and vital work to a group of women in the local church while they golf and live lives of leisure and pleasure! Recall that the New

Testament apostles appointed the "service" ministries in the church of Christ to such as deacons, not so that the apostles could be at ease in Zion, but so that they could give themselves fully to the work of prayer and the word (Acts 6:1-4). It is evident by this passage that the apostles understood their role and knew what it would take in order for sanctification, holiness, and power to manifest. This truth helps us to understand with clarity the role and true responsibility of the intercessor:

"The knee that bows shapes our world." – Prophet Shakespeare

Is intercession a calling for a few specially endowed individuals, is it a supernatural burden, or the natural out birth of our salvation through Christ Jesus our Lord?

THE CALLING IN QUESTION

Permit me to begin this chapter with a discussion of the call of God and the ways that God and self call saints to ministry. I believe that examining the various ways that people have entered ministry will help us identify the *call* or *burden* of intercessory prayer.

First, there is the divine calling of the Lord with which most believers are familiar, whereby an individual hears the voice of the Lord audibly. Next, there is the individual who not only hears but also sees by way of theophany (the Lord appearing in different forms). Both of these are clearly seen in Scripture as one examines the calling of persons such as Adam (Genesis 3:9). Adam hears the voice of the Lord calling but sees no one. Then there is Genesis 6:13-22 and Genesis 12:1-4 where Abraham hears the voice of the Lord but sees no one. In Exodus 3:1 – 4:17, Moses saw the theophany of the burning bush and heard the voice of the Lord. When the Lord appears in a theophany, there is usually dialogue between God and the person to whom He has revealed himself. One can also examine the call of other biblical characters, especially the prophets.

In the New Testament, the calling in the gospels and Acts comes directly from the Lord Jesus to his disciples (i.e. Matthew 4:18-21). These callings also are classified as divine because of the Christnos anointing that was upon and in Jesus, He himself being the fullness of the Godhead bodily (Colossians 2:9). In Acts 9:1-6, the glorified and ascended Lord Jesus appeared to Saul of Tarsus on the road to Damascus. There Jesus revealed to Saul that He was the resurrected Lord and King and called the apostle into a glorious ministry. All of these callings have the stamp of the divine.

Men and women of God are also motivated to ministry by their own desire to serve the Lord and His kingdom. Many have been placed in ministry without the mediation and intervention of our Lord. Recall that when His disciples found persons whom the Lord had not *called* (as they were *called*) casting out demons in His name, they advised Jesus that they forbade the activity. Jesus responded, however, that the work should continue – *"Forbid [him] not: for he that is not against us is for us"* (Luke 9:50). Jesus gave them liberty because of their right intent.

Some saints *call* themselves or someone else encourages or appoints them to a particular ministry. Our motivation or intent for being in ministry, no matter the assignment, is most vital to Christ our Lord. *"For [the Lord seeth] not as man seeth; for man looketh on the outward appearance, but the LORD looketh on the heart"* (1 Samuel 16:7). Many men have gone out with spiritual gifting and anointing but were held back by heaven because of the true intent of their hearts. For the Bible says that *"many are called, but few are chosen"* (Matthew 22:14). All of the elect people of God have received a "general call" to salvation, service and good works, but only certain saints have received or exercise the "special call" to a specific work.

The purpose of examining the call is to determine whether intercession is a *called* work, more specifically a divine calling from God. I suggest that it is not biblical to say that one has been *called* to the "office" or "ministry of intercession" because there is no scriptural support for this assertion. The ministry of intercession in my personal opinion is one of, if not the most, necessary ministries in the Body of Christ, but we must understand that it is not a ministry that stands alone as a calling such as preaching, teaching or any of the five-fold gifts. It is, however, a ministry that should be set in motion within the local assembly by whoever is the apostolic or prophetic voice of that church. This vital ministry should not be toyed with, and those who are placed over a local body's intercessory prayer ministry should receive their appointment as a call of God *through* their man or woman of God (pastor). The intercessors must understand that they influence the life, health and wealth of the church or ministry. If there is no divine unction to function as an intercessor, the person under consideration should not accept this role in his/her church. Pastors should be very prayerful in their selection and appointment of the person who heads the ministry of intercession. One who sounds good praying is not necessarily the one to whom the ministry should be assigned. Criteria must be set in place for the person who leads people to the throne of God. The Bible says that whom the Lord calls He qualifies. Likewise must the pastor qualify the person he or she calls and appoints to this powerful position that moves the hand of the Almighty.

"The prayer that reaches the ear of God also moves His hand." - Prophet Shakespeare

It is Christologically clear that the person who is assigned this task must have the *burden* of Jesus Christ. If there is a *call* to intercessory prayer, it is the call to be like Jesus in His highly exalted position as our Great Intercessor who ever delights in interceding for His saints (see the Book of Hebrews).

THE BURDEN OF INTERCESSORY PRAYER

The word *burden* is mentioned sixty-nine (69) times in the King James Version of the Bible. In the Hebraic language, the word burden is *massa* and in Greek it is *phortion,* meaning a task or service, something carried as cargo in a ship, to be laden. Therefore, when an individual feels what has been interpreted as a calling to intercessory prayer and other areas of ministry, it is not necessarily a divine calling, but rather a burden that has been placed upon them by the Holy Spirit. Just like any natural burden, there are various weights of burden as well as various distances and time that each burden must be carried.

Some men and women of God have been burdened with a message that God intended for them to deliver only one time in one place to one specific people or person, yet the weight of the burden caused them to confess a calling to ministry that the Lord never intended. This type of one time burden that is misinterpreted as a calling to life-long ministry may result in frustration. We would be wise to follow the examples of the prophet Amos and Obadiah. Amos had one message for one particular people and after the message was delivered, his work as a prophet ceased. He was burdened with a message from God to the people of God one time and one time only. Likewise, the prophet Obadiah had one message and no more.

Let us use as an illustration Matthew 28:1-10. There, the risen Jesus instructed Mary Magdelene and the other Mary to *"go and tell my brethren to go to Galilee, and there they will see me"* – this was a one time message to specific people. I am sure that this was a great and exciting burden to carry and deliver but it falls very short of a calling into a life-long ministry. Nor should the interpreter use this as a "proof text" to support women being called to preach the gospel. (Just for the record, Prophet Shakespeare has no problem at all with women in ministry; I have licensed and ordained women for years.)

Conversely, however, can a *burden* translate into a life-long task? Certainly! The Holy Spirit cannot and should not be limited in any area, for He is God and His responsibility is to distribute spiritual gifts for use in the body of Christ (1 Corinthians 12). A burden is often birthed through compassion and concern. The gospel accounts of the ministry of Christ reveal that the compassion of Christ Jesus often motivated Him to heal the sick and even raise the dead (i.e., Matthew 9:35 – 10:1; 14:14). The heart of every believer should be filled with the compassion of our Lord. Note that the root word in compassion is "passion." True compassion comes from agape love, that unconditional love that results in a burden for people you don't know, you don't talk to, you have no real contact with, but because the "burden" is there, you get involved. For many saints that "involvement" is prayer. Sometimes it is a one time prayer occurrence. In other situations, it could cause you to pray endlessly and repeatedly. These types of burdens are what I identify as "A.B.A." (a burdensome assignment) that the Holy Spirit weighs one down with until in the wee hours of the night you can't sleep until you have fallen on your face in prayer, until tears are flowing from your eyes about people, children, nations, churches, etc. that you don't even know. Some of the burdens spring from a prophetic revelation, such as a vision of the face or a young girl who is being abused, visions of calamities, devastations and catastrophic occurrences, and all you can do in response to this knowledge is pray. I remember when I was much younger as a Christian that I would be driving or walking and would pass a school (either full of children or empty) and the burden of prayer would come on me so intensely that I would pull the car over and pray, sobbing uncontrollably for the salvation of the children and their families, for protection from the Lord from predators of every sort, from the influence of the god of this world.

The burden is seen throughout Scripture on individuals with and without a divine or prophetic calling on their lives. In Genesis, Abraham was burdened to pray for a son when he had no heir. In 1 Samuel, Hannah prayed for a son when she saw that she was barren. Barrenness was an incredible burden on a young married woman in her historical-cultural setting because of the philosophical viewpoint of her day and time. In Hannah's culture, a woman's worth and blessing were directly tied to her ability to conceive and deliver children. Nehemiah received an awesome burden after hearing the news of the condition of Jerusalem that inspired him to fast and pray with weeping and mourning for many days (Nehemiah 1:4-11). In Ezra 1:1 ff., the Lord burdened a pagan king named Cyrus to rebuild the temple in Jerusalem after it was destroyed by King Nebuchadnezzar and the Babylonian army.

Throughout the Psalms one can see the cause, effect and results of the many burdens that led the psalmists to pray, praise and worship God in their songwriting. The Psalms are wonderful for the interpretive eye to observe the various levels of burdens and the way they were inspired by the Holy Spirit to give us a greater understanding of His wonderful working with man. Such a study brings illumination to King David's profound question in Psalm 8 – *"What is man that thou art mindful of him, or the son of man that thou visiteth him?"*

Why the burden? The answer comes back to us in biblical, speculative and what I call experiential theology. It is biblically clear that upon giving dominion to man in the creative act in Genesis 1:26-27 that God puts forth His hand or His involvement in the affairs of man without an invitation. However, in order for the Lord to get His will accomplished in the earth realm, He involves and invites persons to make their requests known unto Him. And when we pray with the help of the Holy Spirit (Romans 8), we pray about our own personal concerns and desires, but at the same time we pray the will of God that He has burdened us with – that His word might be fulfilled or made manifest in the natural realm.

This can be clearly seen in Daniel 9:1-19. In verse one Daniel says that he understood through books the number of years that the prophet Jeremiah had specified that the children of Israel were supposed to be in captivity or exile in slavery in Babylon. Daniel found out that the time for liberation according to the prophetic word of God by Jeremiah was overdue. In other words, the prison term for them was up but they were still in jail, still in slavery. God sent them in and only God could bring them out. This revelation knowledge caused a spontaneous burden to ignite in Daniel's heart which resulted in the fervent intercessory prayer found in Daniel 9, the prayer that no doubt moved the heart of God and caused the manifestation of Israel's freedom from bondage (now take a praise break from reading and scream "it's time to come out" – "We're coming out, coming out, coming out, in Jesus name!").

Allow me to share something out of my personal prayer life. I remember that one day while I was in prayer about the drug-infested community surrounding the church I pastured (there was a drug house directly across the street from the church), as I sought the face of God about the removal of the illegal activity and all that accompanies that lifestyle, after calling the police, the city and other agencies to no avail, I finally cried out to God in tears and asked Him why He permits such things to be, why He doesn't do anything about it? I shall never forget hearing the Lord's voice loud and clear that day when He said to me that "There are a lot of things that I desire to do, but no one has asked me." (See James 4:2-3). In other words, He was saying "I sought a man, someone to stand in the gap who would petition my throne, someone to release me in the earth realm to make it happen." Excited about this revelation, I asked Him to remove that drug house and *one week later, yes, seven days later*, it burned to the ground. Hallelujah for the power of intercessory prayer!

The work of intercessory prayer is a burdensome one for those of us who embrace it and make ourselves available to the Holy Spirit for this most serious assignment. Living a life of prayer on behalf of others should be something that every one of us is engaged in. All of us share in the responsibility of this powerful ministry. However, everyone is not conditioned to receive the burden. The Bible says that the *"effectual **fervent** prayer of a **righteous** man availeth much"* (James 5:16, emphasis added). The burden of intercession is reserved for those who are in right standing with God. All saints have the imparted righteousness of God given to us upon the confession of our faith in Jesus Christ. However, there is also the practical righteousness of a sincere, *disciplined* life – the life that we *choose* to live as unto the Lord. One must be fashioned by the Spirit of Christ resulting in a renewed mind, whereby our thoughts and manner of lifestyle have come under subjection to Christ (Romans 12:1-2). The intercessor must be filled with the indwelling Holy Spirit who, according to Romans 8:26, assists us where we are weak (i.e. in our prayer life). He also causes us to mature in the fruit of the Spirit (Galatians 5:22-23), one of the outgrowths being self-control or temperance, causing us to have evidence of being *"partakers of the divine nature"* (2 Peter 1:1-11), having put on Christ. Through the knowledge of what was/is in Him, we will never fall. The intercessor is one who walks in the *favor* of God because of his/her internal resemblance to Christ Jesus our Lord.

I often say in various conversations I have concerning *favor* that God favors those who favor Him and that we must exhibit a two-fold favor – first, that we favor Him within our heart and spirit and secondly, that we favor Him by putting Him first in our lives. Many are not aware of the great favor that God displays by giving such an awesome task to individuals as the burden of being an intercessor. Neither do they understand the blessed prerogatives of the highly-favored intercessor. First, divine protection surrounds the intercessor 24/7. The highly favored person who prays the will of God in the earth realm can truly say in the words of my mother (and the songwriter) "all day and all night angels watching over me my Lord." Secondly, there is divine provision for the intercessor. The Lord will supernaturally care for and provide for the person who takes this assignment to heart. Third, there is a high level of divine communication going on between heaven and the intercessor, for the Holy Spirit of His own choosing, is transmitting the will of God to be prayed either by the direct spiritual burden of mental comprehension, or through the gift of tongues (heavenly prayer language), dreams and visions. For some, there is a combination of these communicative avenues. How ever the burden comes, the obedient, aware and available person who engages in intercession has purchased for him/herself an "open door" to heaven and unlimited access to the throne of Almighty God!

I've come to know through observation, interpretation and personal experience that the making of a genuine intercessor is a perfect work of the Holy Spirit as He fashions the intercessor by purging, pruning, pressuring and pursing him/her for as long as necessary until the humble, sanctified, compassioned and loving life miraculously emerges - from some of the meanest, most hardened, roughest, most selfish sinners the devil had until they fell into the hand of the Lord. What an awesome work He does on us on His potter's wheel and in the refining fire of life!

THE GAPPER'S ANOINTING

The word *gap* is found only one time throughout the entire Old and New Testaments, in Ezekiel 22:30 which reads: *"And I sought for a man among them, that should make up the hedge, and stand in the gap before me for the land, that I should not destroy it. But I found none."* Lower/textual criticism reveals that the man or person described in the text as the "gapper" is one who is blessed and highly favored by God, so that his prayer, posture and position would cause the muscles of God to flex. Let's first look at the gapper's anointed position. It is clear when we look at the persons of God in the Bible that we can stamp with this high and holy title, all were men of God who were called, chosen and sent by God to represent Him before His people in the earth realm. Therefore, it is right for us to declare that they were anointed (i.e. Abraham, Moses, Samuel, King David, just to name a few). Each of these men held a position that reflected their title and their relationship with Yahweh.

Abraham, who we meet as Abram in Genesis 12, was declared a "friend of God" and the "father of the faithful." The Lord imparted or endowed him with "the blessing anointing" which was activated by his obedience to go to a previously unchartered land that the Lord would show him. His faith and act of single-minded obedience made him righteous according to Romans 4:3, causing his prayers to be acceptable before God. The next outstanding feature about Abraham was the relationship that he developed with God. This can be seen not only in the spoken communication between him and Jehovah but also in the fact that he was able to get the angels of the Lord to spend quality time in his tent dining with him (Genesis 18). The person who bears the gapper's anointing is a person who has special favor with God. This is demonstrated by the attention, patience and consideration that God repeatedly gave Abraham as he interceded for Sodom (Genesis 18:16-33). Every time he asked God to consider sparing the city for even the lowest number of righteous person that could be found there, the Lord's reply was one of patience, consideration and favor toward Abraham.

Moses, the emancipating hero of the Bible, even with all of his faults, flaws and failures, was a man of high favor with God because of his obedience. Moses experienced God like no other, from the burning bush calling to the miracles of deliverance in Egypt - the opening of the Red Sea, water from rocks, manna from heaven every day for forty years, quails from the sea - to his "translation" into heaven. This mighty man of God was also one of the greatest intercessors or gappers of the Holy Writ, the only man in the Bible to whom God revealed himself so openly and intimately (showing Moses his back side), revealing unto Him all His glory as He hid him in the cleft of the rocks with His omnipotent hand. Again we see a relationship that develops over the course of years of interaction between God and his prophet Moses, between Lord and servant, maker and messenger, that escalates into something that Moses never dreamed. No one can deny the unlimited favor that Almighty God bestowed upon Moses which catapults him into the hall of fame of biblical antiquities as one of the greatest gappers.

In Exodus 32:30 ff. we find Moses standing in the gap for Abraham's seed because they built and worshipped a golden calf at the mount of God. Moses said to the people, *"You have committed a great sin. So now I will go up to the Lord; perhaps I can make atonement for your sin."* Again, in Numbers 13, after Moses had sent twelve spies to scout out the land of Canaan, ten of them returned with an evil or bad report that the land was too great for them, that heathens and giants were in the land who would destroy them. The people of God did not believe the promises of God and murmured and complained to Moses in anger, even to the point of hatching as assassination plot! In Numbers 14 the Lord spoke to Moses in a solemn tone saying, *"How long will this people provoke me?"* The anger of the Lord was kindled against them to the point that He declared in verse 12, *"I will smite them with the pestilence and disinherit them, and will make of thee (Moses) a greater nation and mightier than they."* Here, like no one else except Jesus dying on the cross, is the gapper's anointing seen shining through the darkness of sin and transgression. Moses had an opportunity to become like Abraham to be the father of a great nation. Yet he chose rather to intercede for his people, to remember the original will of God that was birthed out of love, mercy and grace (v. 13-19), to remind the Lord of His promise to bring the children of Israel out of bondage after 400 years of slavery and return them to the land He gave unto Abraham (Genesis 15:13-16).

A key to a fruitful intercessory life is praying God's word and His will back to Him. The Bible says in Psalm 138:2: *"Thou hast magnified thy word above all thy name."* Again, the word of the Lord says in Matthew 24:35: *"Heaven and earth shall pass away, but my words shall not pass away."* The *guarantee* that God puts on His word is one the intercessor must capitalize on. It is a great asset in prayer. Therefore Moses, because of His position and posture before Jehovah, and his knowledge of the word of God, was able to find divine favor on behalf of Israel resulting in them not suffering total destruction.

All this being said, there is no greater intercessor than our Lord and Savior Jesus Christ. The prophets of old foretold of His divine purpose and position on behalf of fallen man – He willingly served as the propitiation for our sins. Isaiah 53:5 reads: *"But He was wounded for our transgressions, He was bruised for our iniquities; the chastisement for our peace was upon Him and with His stripes we are healed."* The word "but" is an adversative conjunction which serves as a bridge to bring opposites together. The "opposite" is in Isaiah 53:8 - *"For He was cut off out of the land of the living; for the transgression of my people was He stricken."* This prophetic statement by the "eagle-eyed" prophet is called *sensus plenior*, which means the writer was somewhat unaware, or did not or could not possibly understand the ramifications of what he wrote or spoke. Thus, only through a revelation of the Holy Spirit could Isaiah fully understand the vast *gap* that our Lord Jesus filled as He gave His life as an offering for our sins. Jesus' intercessory ministry is far greater than any patriarch or saint. Unlike Abraham and Moses, *only* Jesus hung between two worlds, with blood running down his brow, with pierced hands and feet on an ignominious cross and gave Himself on behalf of us all. His silence and subsequent darkness that filled the earth for three hours on that destined Friday, demonstrated consent, an offering accepted, sacrifice received, and prayer granted. Yes, He the anointed one, stood in the gap for our reconciliation, for our redemption, for our righteousness, for our peace, for our prosperity, so that mercy and justice kissed and created grace. And now, He sits at the right hand of His Father, ever making intercession for the saints (Romans 8:34)!

From Abraham to Jesus, every gapper was anointed, but their anointing as gappers was lodged within the larger *calling* (to ministry) that was upon their lives. In other words, standing in the gap "goes with the turf" when one is called into Christian service.

Every believer who accepts his/her call in life positions him/herself for divine favor – Prophet Shakespeare

It is an absolute automatic that every believer should and can participate in the mediatorial office of Jesus

Christ as our High Priest. In the priestly office, the greatest responsibility is that of intercessor.

A KINGDOM OF INTERCESSORS

Like never before in the history of the church, there is a need for intercessors. The kingdom of heaven is under fierce attack by Satan and his imps and Antichrists are moving all across the world, even as I write. The Bible warns us in vivid symbolic language of the pain and pandemonium that shall certainly and shortly come upon the whole earth (i.e. Matthew 24-25, Revelation). The saints have been instructed to watch and pray (Matthew 26:41; Mark 1313; 14:38; Luke 21:36).

In the Bible *watching* denotes the prophetic; prayer incorporates prophetic awareness. Praying about what is to come, praying for God to move on behalf of his people concerning the things that are about to come upon the world that would affect the saints and the kingdom of heaven, that which would counteract the plans and strategies of the enemy, is part of the spiritual warfare we must wage. Brothers and sisters, it is high time that we awake out of sleep, as the Apostle Paul exhorts us (Romans 13:11), and recognize who we are in God. We are a royal priesthood (1 Peter 2:9) and wealth and riches are a part of the position into which God has placed the saints, but responsibilities accompany rights; priests are also intercessors. The priesthood of the believer is his highest and holiest call, to stand in the gap for a sin-torn world.

We are not just to focus on praying that the saints are blessed. Sin and abomination are rampant all around us. I recently learned that in England homosexual marriage is as legal as a driver's license and that anyone who preaches against homosexuality will be sentenced to jail by a court of law for seven years. We, as the kingdom of heaven, must look prophetically at the word of God and pray against this anti-God, anti-Christ, anti-Christian movement. (One of the goals of the enemy is to do away with the written word of God and doctrinal preaching as we know it.)

It is not by chance that the largest churches in America are built on motivational preaching. But, what would Jesus preach? Would He not challenge the lack of Christian fervor and chastise religious leaders for not teaching and living according to the Word of God? We are called to the priestly office. That makes us a kingdom of intercessors. We are *all* responsible as believers to intercede on behalf of the earth. All of us as citizens of the kingdom of heaven need to look afresh at the ministry of prayer and its importance to the survival of the church and the world. In this season, God is raising up people like Bishop W. H. Murphy, Jr. of the Full Gospel Baptist Church Fellowship International, who heads up FGBCF intercessory prayer ministry, to bring a prayer revival back to the church to restore prayer. Wow!!! What a mind blower, restore prayer where? To the house of God, the place of worship where healing and deliverance is supposed to take place, where demons are supposed to dare to tread and God's Holy Spirit and His holy angels are supposed to abide.

The sad fact is that the church has backslidden, just as it did in the days of Jesus. *"It is written, my house shall be called the house of prayer, but ye have made it a den of thieves."* (Matthew 21:13). We have commercialized the church – our minds are on the money and the money is on our minds. In truth, the mind to pray has left us due to the lack of interest on behalf of "the church" as we know it. We have gone too far. We have departed from our first love (Revelation 2:4). We don't pray for lost souls. We're praying for *our* increase, *our* prosperity. We *may* pray for healing, but we ignore the root issues (demonic influence) which hinder the saints of God. We ignore the warning in Psalm 66: *"If I harbor iniquity in my heart the Lord will not hear me."* The cry of the kingdom of God has not changed – repent, for the kingdom of heaven is at hand (Matthew 3:2)!

In this season, God is building for Himself an army of intercessors who will reclaim the house of God as the house of prayer. This goes beyond the walls of the worship place we visit on Sunday mornings. *"Know ye not that your body is the temple of the Holy Ghost"* (I Corinthians 3:16-17), that we house the Holy Spirit? Saints of God, understand this principle. You are the temple of God Almighty and God is waiting on us to release to Him our prayers and supplications. He's listening to hear that we are in *agreement* with His will, His way. As intercessors, we must understand that it is our responsibility to pray the will of God back to God. A part of the prayer outline that Jesus taught His disciples in Matthew 6 when they asked him *"Lord, teach us to pray"* was *"Thy kingdom come, thy will be done on earth, as it is in heaven."* The will of God is found only in the word of God. We are supposed to pray His word, which is His will, back to Him as it is revealed to us in various circumstances and situations. We are to pray for the coming of His kingdom in the earth – that the government of God, the plan and purposes of God would prevail. Saints, we are the watchers, we are the gatekeepers, we are responsible for what goes on in the earth realm. In Matthew 18, Jesus told the disciples that He has given us the keys to the kingdom. Whatsoever we loose or bind in the earth as priestly intercessors, Jesus will loose or bind in heaven. We, as the kingdom of intercessors, are responsible for the activities of this world.

A Royal Priesthood

To truly understand this most high and holy position or appointment of God by His Spirit, one must have knowledge of the biblical monarchial system. All the kings of Israel had their personal prophets and priests, from the days of Moses until the coming of Jesus Christ. The priests had responsibilities and functions that were assigned to them by a Chief Priest or High Priest. This "head priest" was the greatest one from his brothers (Leviticus 21:10; 2 Chronicles 19:11). The office of High Priest was hereditary, and among many other prerequisites, its holder had to be holy in conduct. Once the High Priest was consecrated to office through an elaborate ceremony of blood sacrifices and anointing of oil, he would be declared sanctified, "the holy one of the Lord" (Psalm 106:16). From this point on, the High Priest had to wear special garments after the order of the priest, with the exception of the outer blue ephod that he wore over his breastplate. Around his hem were pomegranates and bells that would ring as he went into the "most holy place" before the Lord "that he may not die" (Exodus 28:35). On his forehead the High Priest wore "the holy crown" of gold engraved with the words "Holiness to the Lord" (Exodus 28:36-37). Thus, he was represented as bearing the burden of the iniquity of the holy things; he was crowned mediator, intercessor, making atonement for the nation so that God might accept their gifts and show them favor. (Nelson's New Illustrated Bible Dictionary). All priestly garments represented the glory and beauty God placed upon His priests (Exodus 28:4), sanctifying them to minister in His name (Exodus 28:3).

The Old Testament priesthood a symbol or type of that which was to come under the New Covenant and has new life and meaning, as the Apostle declared: *"We are a royal priesthood, a holy nation...."* (1 Peter 2:9). The Apostle Peter was revealing to us that God has made each member of the church, through the blood of Jesus Christ, a High Priest unto Him. We are a *kingdom* of holy priests unto the Lord. He has consecrated us by Jesus' blood. He has anointed us with the oil of the Holy Ghost. He has dressed us in His Word (Ephesians 6:11-18), that we may wage war in prayer as His intercessors!

I cannot overemphasize the importance of every believer's knowing and understanding that *you* are His High Priest in this earth realm. Our lives, our lifestyles, everything about us must please Him, so that our prayers may be accepted, not just for us but for the world and for the kingdom of heaven. That is why it is so important for saints to repent daily, asking God to forgive us our trespasses, even as we forgive others, because this keeps us in a position for our prayers to be made in His (Christ's) righteousness and therefore to be accepted and answered. *"The fervent prayer of the righteous availeth much"* (James 5:16).

Our assignment as priests and intercessors is very crucial to the Lord. We are His representatives in the earth – *"Christ in you the hope of glory"* (Colossians 1:27). God has chosen to *depend on/use* us to accomplish what He wills. He depends on us not only to be burdened with the things of God enough to pray about them, but also to position ourselves to do something about them. I prophesy in this season that God is looking for men and women who want to make a difference in the world in which they live. I hear God saying by His Spirit, I see the good and the evil. I see the drugs, the violence, the crime, the abuse, the government, the broken families, and the church – and I want to get involved. All I need is an *invitation* from the right person, the right intercessor – try me and see what I will do, see what I move by my Spirit, says the Lord of Hosts. Just think of what would happen if the Lord could get just one million of us all around this nation earnestly praying for the same thing at the same time. Church, we would experience breakthroughs, we would see souls saved and people delivered like never before!

The High Priest or the Royal Priest who dwelled in the king's court was often called upon by the king privately to pray over matters that the king requested. We, as a royal priesthood unto the Lord, must make ourselves *available* in prayer, praise and worship to hear and even request in prayer "Lord, what will you have me pray about today? Lord, what is your burden?" We must surrender, like Paul on the road to Damascus during his personal encounter with the Christ, who after receiving the revelation of his sin cried out to the Lord Jesus, "Lord, what will you have me to do?" (Acts 9).

Power is not found in the multitude of flowery words,

but in the secret closet of fervent prayer – Prophet Shakespeare

~

STUDY
GUIDE

~

The Call & Burden of Intercessory Prayer
Study Questions

Introduction

1. What will the restoration of the five-fold ministry restore?

2. Why must prayer be restored?

3. Jesus revealed that real power comes through what kind of prayer?

4. What is an Intercessor?

5. In your own words, explain why prayer must be restored and why apostles appointed deacons for the service ministries in the New Testament.

Chapter 1
1. Explain the divine calling of the Lord that most believers are familiar with?

2. Name two people in the bible that experienced the divine calling of the Lord. Explain the type of divine calling they experienced.

3. Is intercession a divine calling from God?

4. Should intercessors be appointed? If yes, by who and why?

5. In your own words, explain why men and women are motivated to ministry as well as why intercession is one of the most important ministries in the Body of Christ.

NOTES

Chapter 2

1. What is a burden?

2. A burden is often birthed through what?

3. Why does God burden his people?

4. Is everyone conditioned to receive the burden? Why?

5. In your own words, explain the practical righteousness of a sincere, disciplined life, also explain the two-fold favor.

Chapter 3

1. What is a "gapper"?

2. Name three people with the gapper's anointing?

3. What activated Abraham's blessing anointing and made him righteous?

4. What is the key to a fruitful intercessory life?

5. In your own words explain why Moses was known as one of the greatest intercessors/gapper's of the Holy Writ. Explain why every gapper was anointed.

NOTES

Chapter 4

1. Today there a need for intercessors like never before in the history of the church, why?

2. What does prayer incorporate?

3. What is God building for Himself in this season? Why?

4. Explain the spiritual warfare that must be waged by believers. Name some of the sins and abomination believers should focus on in prayer.

5. In your own words, explain the royal priesthood and our assignment as priests and intercessors.

NOTES

Chapter Notes

Chapter Notes

Chapter Notes

Chapter Notes

_____

_____

_____

_____

_____

_____

_____

_____

_____

_____

_____

_____

_____

_____

_____

_____